Against the Odds

Main Features

Page 2 — How did Warren Macdonald survive?

Page 18 — A long wait for rescue

Page 10 — Will Saffi live through the storm?

Page 24 — There are many kinds of courage

Other Features

Recount 8	Diagram 23
Advertisements 9	Flight Plan 30
Log 16	Glossary 31
Letter 17	Index 32

FAST TRACK

COURAGE
The Warren Macdonald Story
Written by Ben Smith

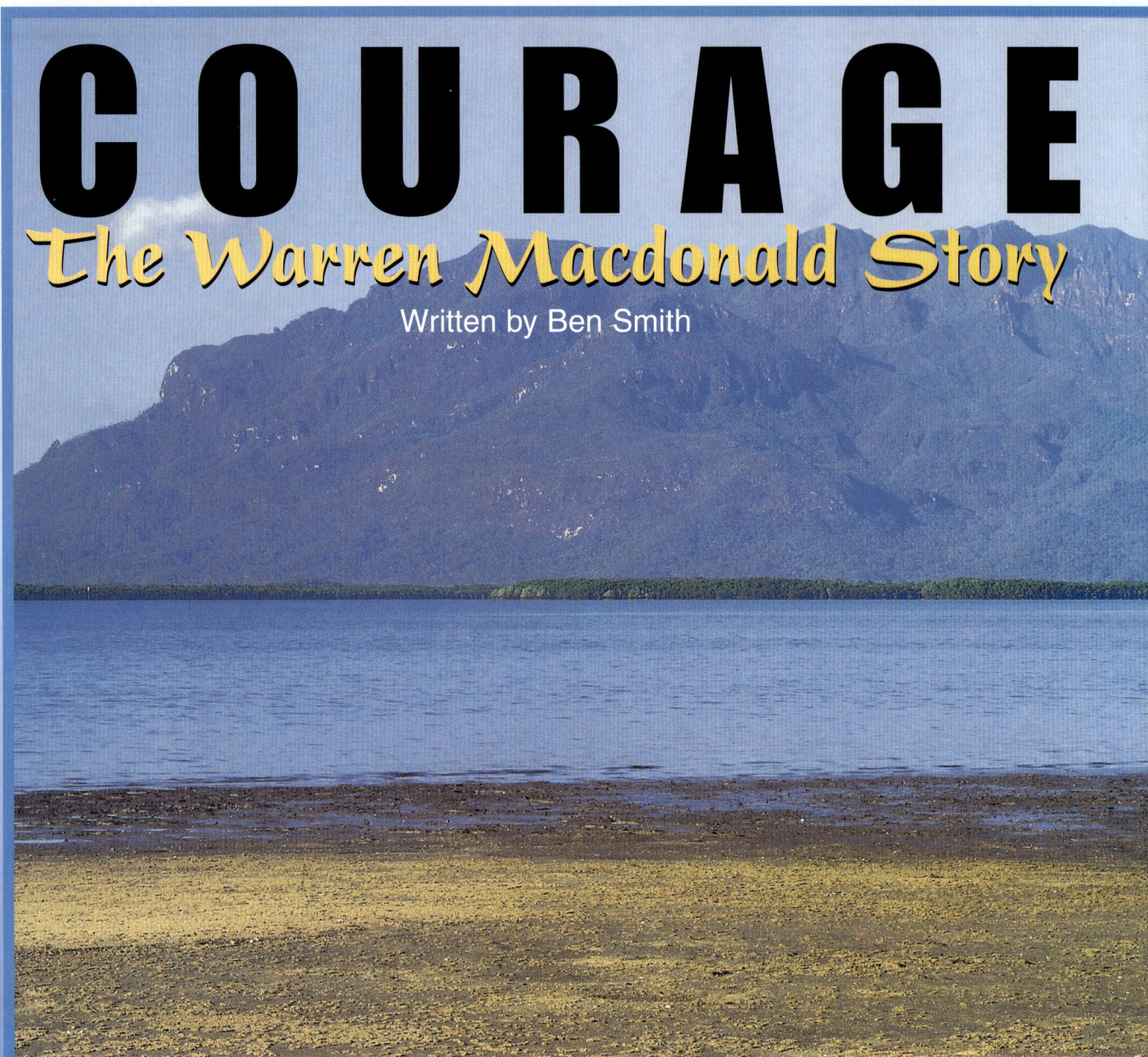

Have you ever wondered what it would be like to be pinned under a rock and not be able to move? Have you ever wondered what it would be like to think that you were going to die? Have you ever wondered what it would be like to lose both your legs?

One man found out. And against the odds, he lived to tell his story. That man is Warren Macdonald.

It happened one day when Warren Macdonald was climbing Mt. Bowen, in Australia. He was climbing with Geert van Keulen, a man he had only just met. Mt. Bowen is not big like Mt. Everest. In fact, you can climb to the top and back down again in two or three days. That was what Warren and Geert were going to do. But, on the first day they turned onto the wrong trail.

The two men made camp. Then Warren went to go to the bathroom. He began climbing over a rock bank by a river, but some of the rocks were loose and he fell into the river. A huge rock fell on him, pinning his legs to the river bottom.

Warren cried out in pain as he tried to get free. Geert heard the cries and came running. Both Geert and Warren struggled to move the huge rock, but they could not. Warren tried not to panic. The pain was **unbearable**.

Climbing Mt. Bowen was supposed to be an adventure, but it almost cost Warren Macdonald his life.

FAST TRACK

The rock was too heavy to push or lift off Warren's legs. The only way to move it was to find something to use as a **lever**. First, Geert thought he would try using a strong branch as a lever. As he ran off to find a branch, it started to rain. Warren had done enough climbing to know that riverbeds can quickly fill up with fast-flowing water when it rains. Again, he tried not to panic.

Geert soon came back with a strong branch. He tried to lift the rock off Warren's legs. But the branch snapped. Next, Geert tried to wedge small rocks under the sides of the huge rock to lift it up. But that didn't work either.

The rain began to fall harder. By now, Warren was tired, soaked, and cold. Geert got Warren's jacket and sleeping bag from the camp. But Warren was too cold to warm up. Soon the water was up to Warren's waist. He thought he was going to drown. His only hope would be if Geert walked out and got help.

In the morning the rain had stopped. Geert got Warren some food and a cup to scoop water from the stream. He propped Warren up with some branches so that he wasn't lying right in the water.

Then, Geert set off down the trail. Warren wasn't sure that he would ever see Geert again. He wasn't sure that he would even live through another night.

> Warren wasn't sure that he would ever see Geert again. He wasn't sure that he would even live through another night.

The day was long. Warren longed for the night so that he could go to sleep and never wake up again. Then night came. Then morning came again, and Warren was still alive. The level of the stream was a lot lower now, and Warren found it hard to get any water in his cup.

Warren just before the accident

Warren was trapped under the rock.

He saw that there was blood in the water. A yabby, which is a freshwater crayfish, was biting his foot! He tried to hit it with a branch, but missed. Then Warren felt a sting and he saw hundreds of ants crawling all over him.

It was then that Warren really thought he was going to die. One of his feet already had green spots on it. The yabby was still biting at his other foot. Ants were crawling all over him and stinging him. He couldn't reach the water with his cup and he was cold.

But Warren wasn't really ready to give up and die. So he kept on hitting out at the yabby and killing the ants. And then, just as his strength was running out, he heard a noise overhead. It was a helicopter. In no time at all, the helicopter crew were lowered down to him on a **winch**.

A doctor looked after Warren while two other men freed him from the rock. They quickly wrapped him in a space blanket to warm him up. Then they strapped him to a stretcher and lifted him up to the helicopter.

FAST TRACK

Warren had beaten the odds. He had survived a bad accident. But Warren Macdonald's story doesn't end there. Both of Warren's legs were amputated above the knee. He had to have further operations to help heal his stumps. The pain was unbearable and Warren often felt like giving up. But he never did.

First, he learned to get in and out of his wheelchair by himself. Then, he had to learn how to walk with artificial legs. Next, he learned to drive a car. And then, against the odds, he decided to climb mountains again.

The mountain Warren chose to climb was Cradle Mountain. It took a lot of **courage** for Warren to use his wheelchair for the first part of the climb. When the trail was too steep, Warren got out of his wheelchair and dragged, pulled, and pushed his body up the mountain using only his arms.

And against the odds, after two long days, he reached the top.

Warren learning how to walk again

Warren had beaten the odds. He had survived a bad accident.

Warren (rear) climbing Cradle Mountain

Against the odds, Warren reached the top.

The summit of Cradle Mountain

GEERT'S STORY

MAN TREKS OVERNIGHT TO SAVE TRAPPED MOUNTAINEER

I had only known Warren Macdonald for a day when we decided to climb Mt. Bowen. We had set up camp for the night. Warren had left the camp to go to the bathroom. Suddenly, I heard him cry out. I ran to where the cry came from. He had fallen and was trapped under a huge rock.

I tried to lever the rock off, but I couldn't. Then I tried jamming smaller rocks under it to lift it up. That didn't work either. I stayed the night with Warren, trying to keep him warm and trying to shelter him from the rain.

In the morning I set off to get help. Going down the mountain was much worse than the climb up. I had to hike through thick forest because the rivers were running high and I could not get over them. I walked into a nest of green tree ants. They bit me all over. I had to jump in the water to get away from them. Another time I slipped down the rocks and fell into some white water. I thought I was going to break my ankles or drown, or both. But I survived. It took me until late that day to get to Little Ramsay Bay. I spent the night on the beach because there were no boats near. The next morning, a boat came. The captain sent a message to the Air Ambulance Service. I told the helicopter crew how to find Warren.

I went to visit Warren in the hospital. I didn't know that they had amputated his legs. I was glad to see that he had beaten the odds.

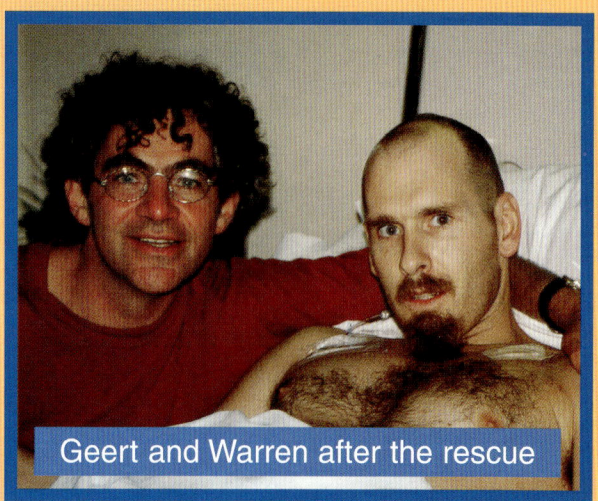
Geert and Warren after the rescue

TRAVEL ADVENTURES

When Was the Last Time You Did Something New?

If you've never tried climbing, come and climb Mt. Bowen with us.

Climbing Mt. Bowen is not difficult. If you are fit and healthy and have a sense of adventure, you will enjoy this climb.

We provide training, guides, tents, camping equipment, and all food.

Check out our web site, or call us to find out more about this adventure.

Hikers' Food

Try Dry Delicacies for all your hikers' food!

We stock a full range of hikers' food. Try us for food that is good to eat, but easy to pack and light to carry. New items are in stock every day.

Specialists in Tents and Sleeping Bags

Come to us for the best prices in town! Some items on sale. Other items at our regular low prices. You won't get a better or cheaper deal anywhere else!

Latest model tents are now in stock. Also, a large range of sleeping bags.

At these low prices you need to act fast!

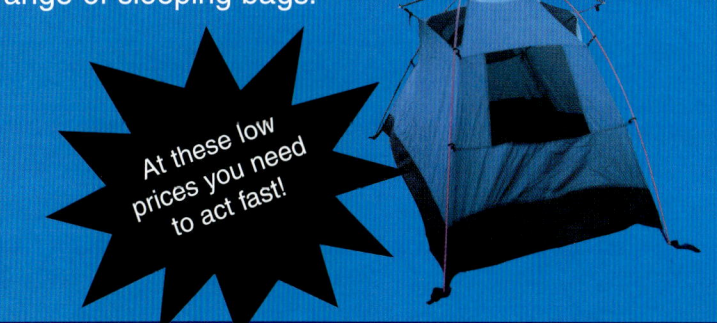

FOR SALE

Men's hiking boots. Size 9. Hard toe. Hardly worn. Already broken in for comfort. Call Tom anytime.

FAST TRACK

And Saffi, Too

Written by Jade Michaels
Illustrated by Kerry Gemmill

It was a beautiful day when the Hewitt family set out in their boat. The water was as flat as a pancake.

Mike, his wife Cinda, and their son Alan liked boating. They went out often, and today they had taken their dog Saffi with them, too.

"Let's go out of the bay to the ocean," said Cinda.

"OK," replied Mike. "We'll take the boat out into the ocean."

"Neat!" yelled Alan. "It'll be neat out on the ocean."

But soon it was not neat out on the ocean. A freak storm blew in. Their boat was thrown all over the place.

10 - REALISTIC FICTION

"Get down!" Mike yelled to Alan as a wave washed over the side of their boat. "Grab Saffi and get below deck!"

"Where did this storm come from?" asked Cinda. "I can't believe it. Fifteen minutes ago it was flat as a pancake."

"I dunno," replied Mike. "But I don't like it."

In no time at all, the waves were higher than the boat. Mike gunned the motor and tried to outrun the storm. Up and down they rolled like they were on a watery roller coaster. And then it happened! One of the waves washed right over the top of the boat. The motor died.

"We'll never get all this water out," yelled Mike to Cinda. "Get Alan and Saffi up here. Quick!"

Cinda ran below deck to get Alan and Saffi while Mike called search and rescue.

▶▶▶

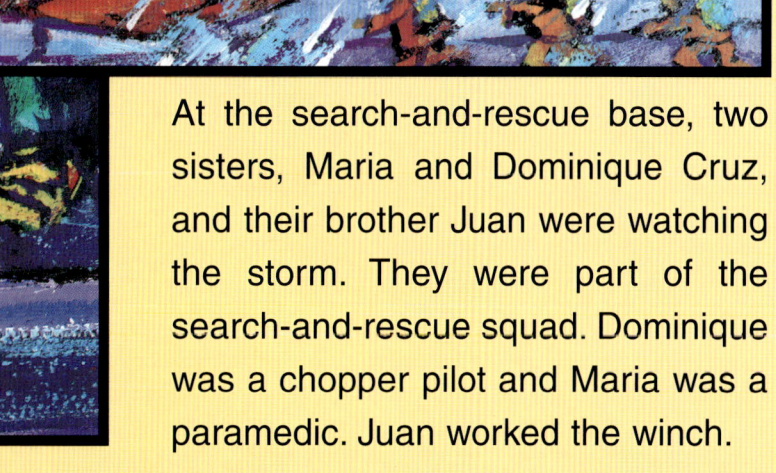

At the search-and-rescue base, two sisters, Maria and Dominique Cruz, and their brother Juan were watching the storm. They were part of the search-and-rescue squad. Dominique was a chopper pilot and Maria was a paramedic. Juan worked the winch.

FAST TRACK

"Where did that freak storm come from?" asked Dominique.

Just as she spoke, the phone rang. Maria answered it.

"A boat is sinking," said Maria as she hung up the phone. "Three people and a dog. Let's go!"

"Do they know where they are?" asked Juan as they ran over to the rescue chopper.

"No," replied Maria. "They're in the ocean, not the bay. I'll call the weather chopper and see if they've seen them. I hope they have."

"Nope, we haven't seen them," said the pilot of the weather chopper. "But we'll take a look and let you know if we see anything."

Back on the Hewitts' boat, things were not good. Each wave sunk the boat lower and it took on more water.

"Just hang on," yelled Mike. "The rescue chopper will be here soon."

"I'm scared, Mike," yelled Cinda, holding Alan tight.

"It's going to be OK," yelled Mike. "Just hang in there."

Just then, another huge wave washed Saffi right off the boat. "Saffi!" screamed Alan. "Saffi's gone!"

"We can't do anything," said Mike. "If we try to get Saffi, we'll drown."

"Do something," cried Alan. "You can't just let Saffi drown. You wouldn't let me drown!"

"We can't do anything," said Cinda, beginning to cry.

All they could do was watch as Saffi bobbed up and down in the waves.

"Saffi!" cried Alan. "Come back!"

"There's the chopper," Mike yelled as another wave washed over them.

▶▶▶

"Can you see anything down there?" asked Dominique.

"Not a thing," replied Maria. "I bet their boat is white."

"It'll be hard to spot a white boat in all those white caps," said Juan.

"Go down lower," said Maria. "I saw something. Yes! I can see them!"

"Got them!" said Dominique as she saw the boat, too. "We don't have a lot of time. That boat's sinking fast."

"I'll get the boy first," said Maria, putting on her harness. "I just hope we're going to be able to make three trips before the boat sinks!"

Dominique lowered the chopper until they were over the boat. Juan lowered Maria down with the winch.

"Any of you hurt?" she shouted.

"We're OK," Mike shouted back.

FAST TRACK

"I'll take the boy first," Maria yelled down to them.

She hooked the harness onto Alan, and Juan lifted them up.

"My dog's in the water," Alan said. "Can you get her?"

"We'll try and do what we can," replied Maria, as she lifted Alan into the chopper.

▶▶▶

Juan lowered Maria down again. More than half the boat was now under the water. Cinda and Mike were hanging on to the rail as tightly as they could. Saffi was still bobbing around in the waves trying to get back to the boat.

"Here she comes again," said Mike. "Get ready, Cinda." Cinda reached out but she couldn't reach Maria.

"Hold on!" said Mike. "I'll hold the rail, you hold my hand. Then she'll be able to reach you."

Cinda held Mike's hand.

"That's it," called Maria. "Just a little more. Got you!"

She looked at Mike. "Be back for you soon," she said. "Hang on!"

But just then, another huge wave hit the boat. The boat sank and Mike was washed into the water!

▶▶▶

"Mike!" screamed Cinda.

"Dad!" screamed Alan.

"It's OK, Alan," said Juan as he pulled Maria and Cinda up. "Maria will go back down for your dad as soon as she has your mother up here. Your dad will be OK."

"He'll drown," screamed Alan. "He and Saffi will drown."

"He'll be OK," said Juan again. "Saffi will be OK, too."

Maria went down again. Saffi was swimming through the waves trying to get to Mike. Just as Maria got the harness on Mike, Saffi somehow jumped into his arms.

"Maria's got them both," shouted Dominique. "Mike has Saffi and Maria has Mike! Against the odds, even Saffi is safe!"

Greater Gull Bay Search-and-Rescue Log

Date and Time	Call	Action Taken
SEPTEMBER 6 0900	Elderly man – heart attack while swimming	Ambulance sent to Sandy Beach. Jim Brown, male, age 74. Heart attack while swimming. Companion pulled him out of the water and began CPR. On arrival, took over CPR. When Mr. Brown was stabilized we took him to Gull Bay Hospital.
1130	Surfer swept onto rocks off Windy Point	Ambulance sent to Windy Point. Lifeguards unable to reach surfer because of strong rip and onshore winds. Paramedics Wheeler and Yakov reach surfer by descending cliffs. Broken leg, plus bruising, and cuts to body. Surfer stabilized before being hauled up the cliff. Taken to Gull Bay Hospital.
1400	Boat with three people and a dog in trouble outside the Bay area. Boat taking on water and sinking.	Chopper sent. Man, woman, child, and dog all winched to safety. No injuries. Man suffering from cold. People taken to Gull Bay Hospital.

12 Cove Street
Gull Bay

September 6

Greater Gull Bay Search and Rescue
Pelican Point
Gull Bay

Dear Maria, Dominique, and Juan,

Mike, Alan, and I would like to thank you very much for saving us last week when our boat sank in the freak storm outside Gull Bay. When we set out that day the weather was so calm we never thought that we would need rescuing.

We are so thankful that you responded to our call so quickly. We know that if you had not rescued us when you did, none of us would be alive today.

We would also like to thank you for saving our dog, Saffi. When she was swept overboard, none of us thought we would ever see her again.

I have enclosed a donation as I know you always need extra funds to keep the search-and-rescue base running.

Thank you again.

Regards,

C. Hewitt

Cinda Hewitt

GULL BAY BANK

TO _Greater Gull Bay Search and Rescue_   06/09/01

AMOUNT _Five Hundred dollars only_ $500

MR. AND MRS. HEWITT   *C. Hewitt*

"09 58" " 12 0094 846" "00"

FAST TRACK

65 HOURS

On July 30, 1997, a massive **landslide** hit the town of Thredbo. This is the story of a heroic rescue.

July 30, 11.37 P.M.

There is a loud roar. Stuart Diver and his wife Sally wake up to find their house crashing in around them. They are buried by a landslide. They are trapped in a space no bigger than a **coffin**.

Sally is trapped by a concrete beam. She is pinned to the bed. Stuart feels water coming into the cavity where they are trapped. He fears that they will drown. He is able to lift himself up a little but he cannot lift Sally because she is trapped under the concrete beam. She drowns. The water drains away and Stuart is left, trapped, alone.

Around Midnight

Police and 20 firefighters arrive. The person in charge of the rescue says the house is too unstable to go into. The landslide may start again and bury the rescuers. They cannot take a chance. They cannot start to rescue Stuart until a scientist says that the house is **stable**.

Written by Sandy Brown

The rescuers had to wait until the site was stable before they could begin.

The landslide caught everyone by surprise.

July 31, 5 A.M.

Paul Featherstone, a paramedic, arrives in Thredbo. He sees what the landslide has done. There is **rubble** everywhere. There are bricks, mud, and concrete all over the place. Cars and trees are upside down. There are big rocks everywhere.

July 31, Sunrise

More than 200 firefighters, police officers, paramedics, and other rescuers arrive. They set up rescue headquarters. The person in charge of the rescue thinks that there must be at least 11 men and 7 women trapped under the landslide.

July 31, 10 A.M.

A team of scientists say that the site of the landslide is stable enough for the rescuers to go into. They arrange a warning of three blasts on a siren if the land becomes unstable again. If the rescuers hear the three siren blasts, they will have to leave the site.

FAST TRACK

July 31, 10:30 A.M.
The rescuers start looking for survivors. They join hands and pass pieces of rubble to trucks. Firefighters crawl over the landslide. They look through the gaps in the rubble and call out to see if anyone answers.

August 1, Sunrise
The rescuers have found only one body. They do not think that anyone else will still be alive. They think that anyone who has not died by now will have frozen to death.

Rescuers working

August 2, 5:30 A.M.
Steve Hirst, a firefighter, hears a voice. He calls out and Stuart Diver answers him. The rescuers start to move the rubble from where they hear Stuart's voice.

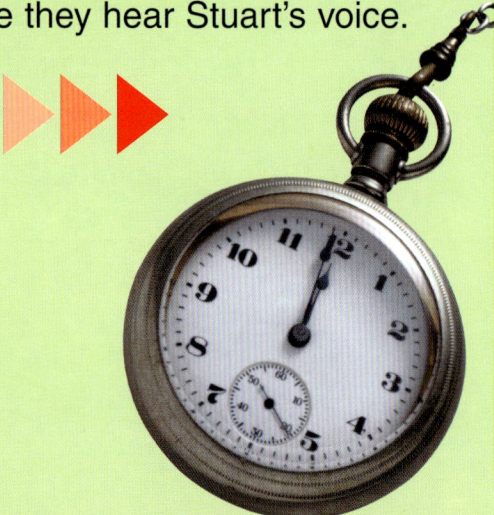

Rescuers moving the rubble

August 2, 6:30 A.M.

The rescuers reach a big slab of concrete. They can hear Stuart's voice more clearly. They keep digging. Steve Hirst and six other rescuers dig through a small gap in the rubble. They keep digging.

August 2, About 9:30 A.M.

Stuart says, "I can see your light." The rescuers have dug through more concrete slabs, but Stuart is still trapped under yet another one.

A firefighter sees Stuart's fingers poking up through a crack. They have reached him at last.

Paul Featherstone crawls into a tunnel and gets as close to the crack as he can. He talks to Stuart. There are three blasts on the siren. Someone drags Paul out of the tunnel. Paul says he is going back in or Stuart could die. He goes back in. Other rescuers keep watch to make sure the part of the site where Paul and Stuart are is stable.

Paul gives Stuart an oxygen mask. He gives Stuart a warm-air hose to put next to his body to keep him warm. He puts a meter on Stuart's thumb so he can tell how fast Stuart's pulse is. He puts a feeding tube into Stuart's mouth. The rescuers cut a hole in the concrete slab above Stuart's feet.

Rescuers lifting concrete slabs from the mudslide.

FAST TRACK

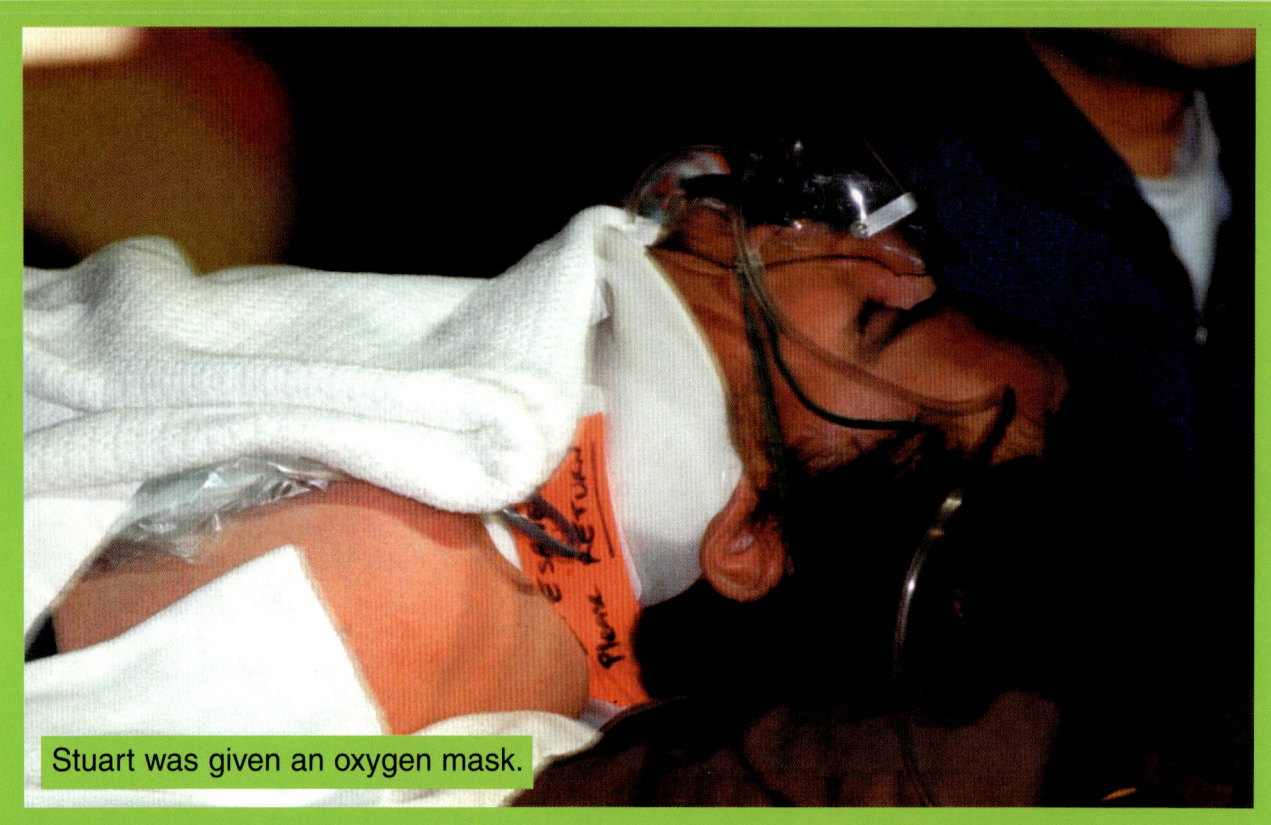

Stuart was given an oxygen mask.

August 2, Three Hours Later

At last the hole that the rescuers have dug is big enough for Paul to get in beside Stuart. A doctor gets in, too. The doctor puts an IV line into Stuart's ankle. Paul puts a harness around Stuart's waist and pulls him, feet first, until his head is under the hole.

August 2, 5:17 P.M.

Two firefighters pull from above. Paul Featherstone and another paramedic hold Stuart under his arms. They pull him to the surface. Stuart is taken to the hospital.

He should be dead. He has been buried alive for 65 hours.

But against all odds, he is alive.

How Stuart Diver Was Saved

1 After digging 8 feet (2.5 m), rescuers realize that Stuart Diver is trapped under another concrete slab.

2 A nourishment tube and a warm air hose are passed to Stuart through the hole.

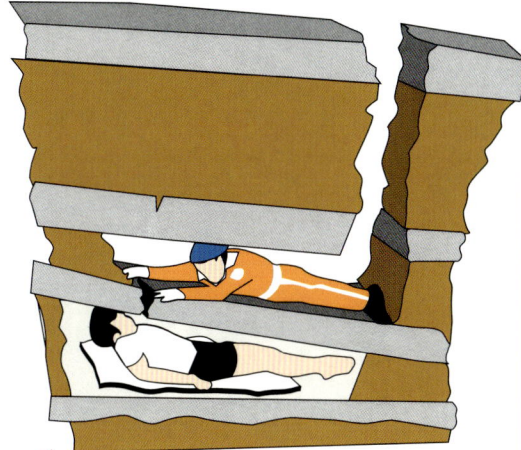

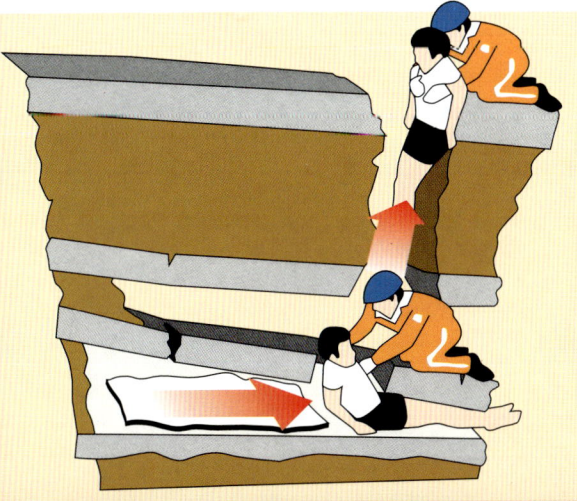

3 Stuart is moved until his head is beneath the hole where his feet were, then lifted to the surface.

FAST TRACK

Abby Flies Again

Written by Cheryl Ryan   Illustrated by Paul Konye

Waking up early in the morning isn't what most teenagers like to do. And Abby wasn't any different from most teenagers when it came to waking up early. She liked sleeping in, especially on weekends. But this weekend was different – she was going to fly in a plane race with her Uncle Todd. So Abby was up early and eager to get going.

Flying was in Abby's blood. She liked flying just about more than anything else she could think of. As well as her uncle, both her dad and her mother were pilots, too.

Abby's Uncle Todd had been flying for years. He had flown hundreds of flights since he was a teenager like Abby. He had also flown in many races because he liked the competition. Abby had flown with him in a lot of races. She had learned to read charts and maps really well.

Abby's father drove her to the airport to meet her uncle. The race began at eight that morning.

Abby and her uncle would fly more than 1,200 miles over two days before the race ended.

When her father dropped Abby off he said, "Good luck. Fly safely. See you in two days."

Soon Abby and Todd were off in their single-engine plane. The weather around the airport was clear and sunny. But, as they headed over the snow-covered mountains, a large bank of billowy clouds had gathered.

FAST TRACK

"What do you think, Abby?" asked Todd. "Should we fly through or around those clouds? They don't look like bad storm clouds, and we can save a lot of time if we fly through them."

Abby looked at the charts and said, "You're right. Going around will add over 100 miles to our flight. It will cost us a lot of time. I think we should go for it and take the shortcut through the clouds."

"OK, Abby," he replied. "We won't see any scenery, but it will be quicker."

They headed into the clouds. The clouds were much thicker than Todd had thought. Abby began to feel a little uneasy. She couldn't see anything through the thick billowy whiteness.

It wasn't long before Todd got worried and said, "I think we've made a mistake, Abby. I'm going to turn around and fly out of here. Now, hang on."

Todd banked the plane steeply to the left. Suddenly the plane began to shake. It dropped down lower in the sky. Then, before Todd could pull the plane up, the left wing struck the top of a tree and ripped off. The plane tumbled violently into the trees. As it tumbled through the trees, the plane broke in half.

Abby's head hit the roof of the plane and she was knocked out. When she woke up, she was lying in the twisted wreckage. She looked around for her uncle. She could see him lying in the snow outside. He wasn't moving!

She cried out, "Uncle Todd! Wake up! Wake up! Please tell me you're OK! Please, don't die!"

But Todd didn't answer. His body just lay there, without moving.

Abby's legs were numb. She couldn't feel them. She tried to stand up, but she couldn't. She knew she was lucky to be alive. But how long could she survive without help? She was so cold.

Abby reached for the radio and tried to call for help. But the radio had broken in the crash. The radio was useless!

But, what Abby didn't know was that two snowshoers, Ben and Amy Gates, were staying in a cabin close by. They heard a plane passing low over the cabin. Then, they heard a crashing sound through the trees.

Ben and Amy set off in the direction of the crashing sound. Within 20 minutes they were at the crash site. First, they saw Todd lying still in the snow. He was dead.

Then, they heard a voice saying, "Help, please help me. I can't move."

As Ben and Amy looked closer, they saw Abby tangled in the wreckage of the plane.

"My legs are numb. I can't feel my legs, and I can't stand up," said Abby, sounding very scared.

FAST TRACK

"Don't worry. Try not to move," said Ben as he tried to comfort Abby. "Use the cell phone and call for help," he said to Amy.

Fuel was seeping out of the plane and there were sparks coming from some broken wires. Ben and Amy knew they shouldn't move someone who was hurt, but they were worried about fire. Very carefully, they lifted Abby and carried her away from the wreck.

The next hour seemed to last a very long time. Then, they spotted a rescue helicopter! The rescue helicopter had arrived! Soon, Abby was on board and flying to a hospital. Doctors and nurses and her parents were waiting for her.

The doctors got to work. Abby's spine was X-rayed. The doctors' worst fears were right. Two vertebrae were crushed and the spinal cord was damaged. Telling Abby and her parents the bad news was very difficult. The doctors said that Abby would probably never walk again. But Abby was thankful to be alive. She was determined not to feel sorry for herself.

"I may never walk again," she said, "but don't bet that I will never fly."

It wasn't long before Abby was going to physical therapy. She worked hard to make her arms strong. She needed to use her arms to get in and out of her wheelchair and to be able to climb into the cabin of a plane.

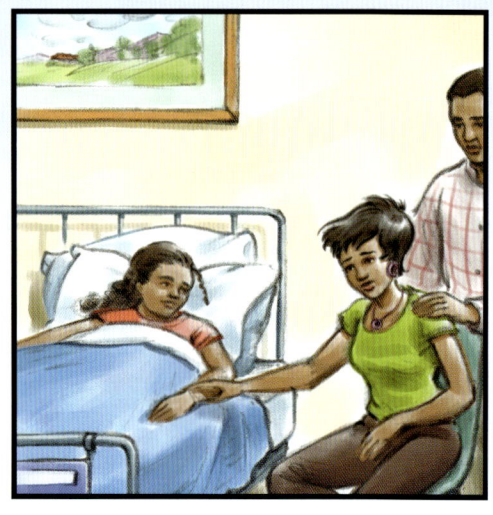

Two months after the accident, Abby's father took her back to the airport so she could fly with him.

"Are you sure you want to go up?" he asked her.

"Are you serious? Yes! Yes, I do. More than anything!" she said. And so, for the first time since the crash, Abby went up into the air. And she loved it.

"How about we get you signed up for flying lessons," her father said. "If your dream is to fly, then let's make it come true."

So Abby learned to fly. She had to take many hours' worth of lessons and get a medical certificate saying she would be OK flying. Her plane had to be specially fitted inside so that she could use all the controls.

It took her two years to learn to fly. But, by the time she was 20, she was one of the best pilots around! That year, she won a 2,500-mile coast-to-coast plane race in record time. She was the first woman pilot to win the race. And her time was better than anyone's who had ever won the race.

Abby had won against the odds. She proved that a strong will can beat even the biggest obstacles.

FLIGHT PLAN

GTE DUAT USERNAME	GTE DUAT PASSWORD
Abby Smith	Piper One

1. Type	2. Aircraft Identification	3. Aircraft Type/Special Equipment	4. True Airspeed	5. Departure Point	6. Departure Time	7. Cruising Altitude
✓ VFR ○ IFR	XX5	yes	140 KTS	LAX	0930 Proposed (Z)	5,000A

8. Destination (Airport Terminal Code)	9. Est. Time En Route		10. Remarks
SJX	Hours: 3	Minutes: 10	N/A

11. Fuel on Board	12. Alternate Airport(s)	13. Pilot's Name, Address, Telephone Number & Home Base Terminal Code	14. Number of Aircraft
Hours/Minutes 4 30	SFX	Pilots Name: Abby Smith Address: 1 Brown Ave Phone: 555-1694 Destination Contact: Stefan Smith Destination Phone: 555-1121 Aircraft Home Base Terminal Code: LAX	64
			15. Color of Aircraft: Blue

GLOSSARY

GLOSSARY for *Courage*

courage – Finishing a task or action knowing that it is difficult or dangerous.

It took great **courage** to save the children from the burning house.

lever – Any type of bar that can be used to lift things up, or pry things open.

Angela slid the **lever** under the slab and then pushed down, causing the slab to lift off the ground.

unbearable – Something that cannot be suffered or endured.

The pain was so **unbearable,** he thought he was going to die.

winch – A tool that is used to lower or drag other objects. It is usually made up of a small motor and a metal cable.

The life preserver was hooked onto the end of the **winch** cable, and the young man was winched into the chopper.

GLOSSARY for *65 Hours*

coffin – A long narrow box that people are buried in.

The **coffin** was lowered into the ground at the end of the funeral service.

landslide – Rain-drenched dirt that usually slides down a hill or mountain because it can no longer stick to the surface of the Earth.

The **landslide** came down the mountain and swept away the whole town.

rubble – Loose and uneven bits of rock, concrete, or other materials.

The explosion left a large pile of **rubble** in the road where the car used to be.

stable – Something that is steady and balanced.

The building was **stable**, even though there had just been an earthquake.

INDEX

accident	3–6,16
amputation	6,8
ants	5,8
Diver, Sally	18
Diver, Stuart	18, 20–23
doctor	5
Featherstone, Paul	19,21,22
firefighter(s)	18–22
helicopter	5,8,16
hiking	8
Hirst, Steve	20,21
Keulen, Geert van	3,4,8
landslide	18
Macdonald, Warren	2–8
mountains:	3,18
Cradle Mountain	6,7
mountain climbing	3
Mt. Bowen	3,8,9
Mt. Everest	3
paramedic(s)	16,19,22
police	18
rescue(s)	5,16,18–23
search and rescue	16,17
survivor(s)	20
Thredbo	18,19
wheelchair	6
yabby	5